DESIGNING FOR LEADLIGHTS

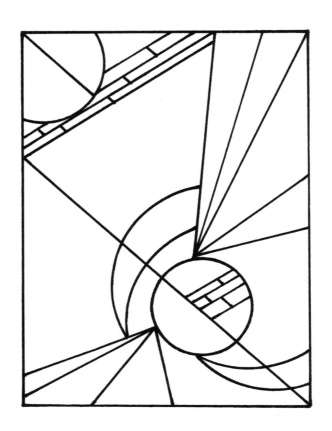

DESIGNING FOR LEADLIGHTS

Will Fraser

Kangaroo Press

Acknowledgments
The author acknowledges with gratitude the advice and assistance
from many sources, coupled with his own 15 years experience at
the hands of his mentors, in the compilation of this book.

First published in 1994 by Kangaroo Press Pty Ltd
3 Whitehall Road Kenthurst NSW 2156 Australia
PO Box 6125 Dural Delivery Centre NSW 2158
Typeset by GT Setters Pty Limited
Printed in Hong Kong through Colorcraft Ltd

ISBN 0 86417 578 7

CONTENTS

FOREWORD

Following the success of my earlier book *Pictures In Glass* it seemed a natural progression to prepare a straight-forward work on the actual technique of designing for leadlights. For although it is quite satisfactory for beginners to copy patterns direct from the host of leadlight books currently on the market, the fullest satisfaction of working in glass may only be realised when you actually work out and create leadlight designs of your own.

Many leadlight enthusiasts seem unaware of the latent design skills which so many of them possess, perhaps also believing that original designing is an area which is beyond them.

Nothing could be further from the truth.

The purpose of this book therefore is to show you, in an uncomplicated way, how to design your leadlights so as to achieve the best possible results from your own imagination.

As you progress in your designing you will find that you begin to acquire your own style—that personal creative quality which makes your own leadlights different from all others.

It is this creative individuality and freedom of spiritual expression which continues to make leadlighting one of the world's fastest growing and most popular visual art mediums.

Designing for leadlights is a stimulating pastime, calling for originality, creative balance, and a well developed sense of colour and line.

Designing for Leadlights contains all you need to know to become proficient at this skill, together with a selection of original drawings and photographs which help to further illustrate the world of designed leadlights.

Chapters 6 and 7 are devoted to 28 new designs in full-page format, while 15 more are scattered throughout the text.

My thanks to all those friends who have aided me in my creative work over the years, and in particular to Enid Bain and José de Koster for their invaluable ongoing support.

My thanks also to Tony Stafrace, of The Melbourne Glass Centre, for his enthusiastic assistance in this project.

A professional design service, offering original drawings to suit your own leadlight requirements, is available from:

Will Fraser Leadlights
83 Duke Street
Castlemaine Victoria 3450 Australia

1 CREATIVITY

Creative—*characterised by originality of thought or inventiveness . . . having or showing imagination . . .*

Creativity is something of a dynamic process—a natural ability which all of us once possessed and practised freely as children. The creative spontaneity of youngsters plays an important part in their development, often expressing a deep, spiritual consciousness not yet fully understood by those so young and inexperienced in an adult world.

What happens to that spontaneous, creative spirit as we grow older and why is it that a formerly regular and enjoyable release of creative energy is no longer deemed important or necessary by so many adults?

The answer lies largely in our conditioning. As children, no hard-and-fast concepts have yet had a chance to become imposed on our young minds and so we are free to express ourselves as we truly feel and see fit. The older a child becomes the more he or she absorbs the whole gamut of imposed adult rules and concepts, finally becoming 'conditioned' to fit into society and the environment.

Unfortunately, from a creative point of view, the more a child is conditioned the more at risk its inner creative centre becomes until eventually, what once seemed like spontaneous creative fun no longer appears relevant or acceptable in a grown-up society.

Creativity is *not* something that one 'used to do' as a child! And it is *not* something which one naturally 'grows out of' as one gets older!

On the contrary, creativity is an important part of life, and may yet prove to be a vital component, without which human beings find it difficult to function in a truly balanced and harmonious way.

Today it is more important than ever before that personal creativity be fostered and developed at all levels of society in order to re-aquaint individuals with their intrinsic inner selves. It is this inner self that almost demands expression in some creative form in order to fulfil the individual's oneness with life itself.

The fact that creativity represents a strong and positive energy makes it an important and vital force in a world which is showing increasing signs of bureaucracy and negativity.

How exactly does one go about becoming 'deconditioned' to get back in touch with that vital inner creative centre? The answer lies in consciously setting out to practice simple awareness techniques which will re-kindle and foster creative expression and to always keep in mind that thoughtless uniformity never creates anything . . .

Here are some pointers on understanding how to become more creative.

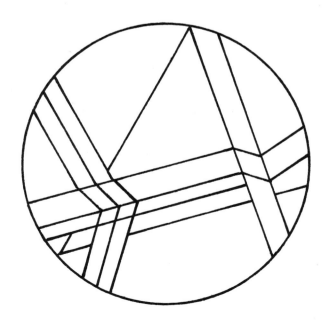

Doing

By doing one becomes motivated, extending purely intellectual ideas onto an experiential level where they often take on a life of their own and lead to other things.

Doing provides *stimulation* which in turn quickens the senses and provides *a form of creative energy*.

Merely thinking about wanting to be more creative is not enough.

You have to *do* something about it.

You have to *act*.

And creativity leads directly to *increased creative awareness*.

Looking

As you become more motivated to *do*, you should at the same time be cultivating the art of *looking*.

Books, exhibitions, magazines, television, newspapers and videos all provide a fertile source of visual contact and mental stimulation. Visiting art galleries is often a very good way of developing a creative feeling and understanding of things, helping you to get back in touch with your own inventive creative centre.

Make sure you see (and *look* at) as many leadlight exhibitions as you can and, as you get about, pay close attention to the thousands of old leadlights to be seen in houses of every style and shape all over the country. Note which of the old leadlight design styles appeal to you, and keep a sketchbook to record the more unusual or original patterns you come across in your travels. Take photographs of the best leadlights you see to form a useful photographic record for future reference and ideas.

will increase. As your output grows so will your drawing quality, your own creativity and, as a result, the originality of your work.

Later you can go back to your book of rough sketches and start designing *in detail* the best of what you have drawn.

Subject focusing

Every day, in the course of our normal activities, we encounter literally hundreds of 'normal' objects, ranging perhaps from a magnificent stand of trees to the charming ruins of some old cottage or building.

Becoming sensitive to the individual qualities of the things you see is of great importance as an increased awareness of form and pattern within the environment leads to a more creative approach to design.

By focusing on everyday objects you will learn to be able to *simplify* their forms so that they can be reproduced more easily into leadlight designs. Focusing merely means half-squinting the eyes when looking at an object so that its form becomes more definite, harder-edged.

Drawing

It is always a good idea to keep a sketch pad close by in which you can put down all your ideas for designs. Unless you record design ideas the moment they pop into your head, chances are you will either forget them, or the original shapes will become blurred and lost with the passing of time, or become something quite different.

Make it an enjoyable, creative habit to sketch regularly. Don't try for perfection to begin with, rather stay relaxed and design as often as time permits. The more you draw the more you will experience and the more your output

Figure 1.1 Focusing on your subject enables you to eliminate detail and simply draw in the basics of shape and design

By doing this you can reduce the object you are looking at to its *basic* characteristics, eliminating confusing detail (see Figure 1.1). Designing for leadlights makes use of basic form, the lines later becoming lead lines in the finished panel.

When using this focusing technique, always distinguish the main (dominant) parts of the studied object and start your rough sketch drawing these first, adding necessary detail later.

Trees, flowers, rocks, animals, landscapes, the sea, forests, can all be 'reduced' by focusing and re-drawn in a simplified form which still resembles the object being portrayed.

Copying

Most people start out in leadlights by copying from commercial patterns available in the many books currently on the market. It is an excellent way to develop a 'feel' for lines and form as virtually any image of sufficient interest can be copied and used. Copying is perhaps best seen as an aid, as using another's design rarely satisfies the creative inner you and does not, long-term, contribute to original, personal creative growth.

Usually, the stage you next go through after direct copying is *changing* what you have copied into something different, something you feel would look better than the original.

Once you begin doing this on a regular basis you are well on the way to designing for yourself. Eventually you will not need other people's patterns at all, preferring instead the challenge of designing your own.

Getting ideas

Virtually everything around us represents an idea, or was one to begin with.

Ideas for leadlight designs can come literally from anywhere, at any time; providing you jot them down you should never be short of inspirational material. Visual mediums such as art, television, motion pictures and videos, and what each of us 'sees' in the course of a normal day, all provide good and varied sources for creative ideas. Perhaps the shape of a piece of ultra-modern Italian furniture, or some rare, exotic flower being featured on a television gardening show could be the spark—the list of sources is endless.

What is important is that you become visually and mentally *aware* of things and always ready to *translate* what you 'see' into designs. Books, especially pictorial works on art and decor, are also excellent sources of visual stimulation and ideas for the would-be designer.

First you have to *create*; from creating will come *skill*.

2 ELEMENTS OF DESIGN

Most simply expressed, design is the breaking up of a set space into other shapes and areas.

There are two main sources of inspirational ideas for design; nature and geometrics.

- Nature's many facets offer a virtually unlimited source for ideas and motifs and include animal and plant forms, water, fire, sun, wind, sea . . .
- Geometrics makes use of the many lines, planes, rectangles, triangles, circles and other shapes which can be worked into unlimited networks of more formalised designs.

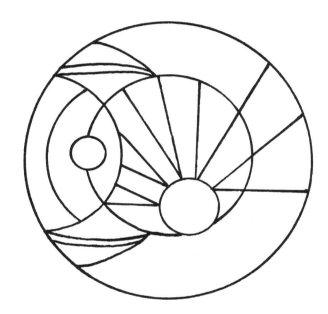

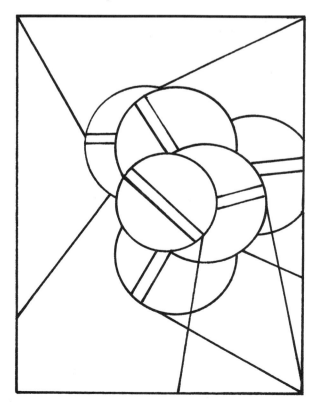

Design contains five basic elements:
Line Indicating the direction or form
Form The outward visible shape of an object
Tone Either light or dark
Colour Any hue other than black, white, or grey
Texture The surface quality of the object

Design also has five basic principles of arrangement:
Repetition The recurrence of an element
Rhythm The grouping of the elements in relation to one another
Balance The harmonising of elements with one another
Proportion The comparative relationship of sizes and shapes
Emphasis The focal point

Before you start thinking about designing a panel of your own it would be a sound idea to first read and thoroughly absorb the following general pointers on design.

The subject

Choosing a subject is the very first step in any designing. Any subject, object or shape can be chosen to feature in your panel.

A designer will usually select a subject which is in harmony with the immediate environment where the completed leadlight will be on display.

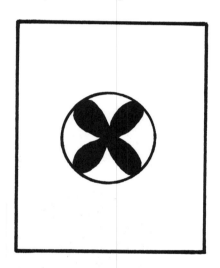

The background

This is the area into which the subject is placed. *It is always equal to the shape and size of the panel being designed.*

The background space can be altered visually by placing the subject in it in a variety of positions. As an example, draw a rectangular background using a piece of white paper; then cut out a small motif (the subject) using dark paper, and place the dark motif onto the background.

The motif now relates to the background.

Moving the motif around inside the rectangular background will change the overall visual impact of the design (see Figure 2.1). Notice how the dark motif relates to the edges of the white background. Does the motif appear to be too close to an edge? Is the motif visually stable, or is it just stuck there awkwardly against the background?

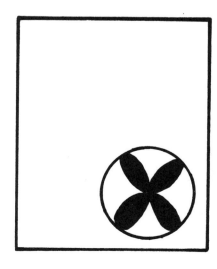

Figure 2.1 The subject (decorative circle) placed in different locations in the white background gives different visual effects

Now look hard at the dark motif within the background to work out different positions for it and discover new design possibilities, new perspectives.

Perhaps there is *one* position that you think looks best for the motif. If so, this is the *right* position for you and your own design attitude. Someone else may choose another position for the motif which feels right for them.

In the end designing for leadlights is a very personal thing so there is really no correct end result. Rather it is what the individual designer is finally happy with. The end result must be what the designer thinks works in relation to how he/she originally visualised the impact of the design.

It should be stressed, however, that no matter how personal your finished design is, it should always contain the five basic principles of design arrangement mentioned on page 11.

Interplay of figure and background

Increasing the size of your subject within its background will immediately introduce new ideas into your design (see Figure 2.2).

Try experimenting yourself, using a large dark motif and placing it on a white rectangular background. Observe how the whole visual concept of the design changes the larger the dark motif becomes.

By using a very large dark motif on your background you will note that the motif itself has taken over and now dominates the white background, which in turn recedes visually.

You could look also at the changes that may occur when you enlarge a design. Sometimes its whole character changes. Is the design still visually pleasing? Has it become too strong? Too weak?

Figure 2.2
The subject now dominates the background space, which has receded into insignificance

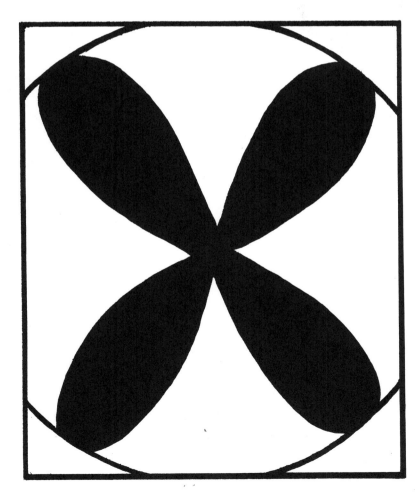

Figure 2.3 Changes in size may also affect the design's character

Balance

A symmetrical design

All the shapes in any design have what is known as *substance*. When these shapes are distributed onto a background they form relationships which look and feel either *balanced* or *unbalanced*.

A balanced design, in which one half of the shapes look exactly the same as the other half, is called a *symmetrical design* (see Figure 2.3). When this balance comes from a single central point it is known as a *radially symmetrical* design (see Figure 2.3).

A design can be balanced even when one side doesn't look like the other; here the visual feel and distribution of the combined shapes balance each other. This is especially true of abstract shapes (see Figure 2.3).

Abstract designs often deliberately feature radical and seemingly unharmonious shapes but, by thoughtful use of lead lines, and repeating strong colours, the visual substance of the design appears balanced.

A radially symmetrical design

Figure 2.3

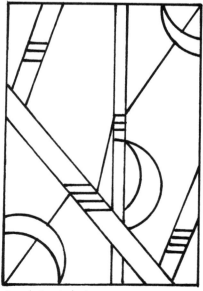

An abstract design

Space

The *space* around a figure or group of figures is as important to the balanced design as the actual figures themselves. It is very important that the design and structure of the lead lines in the background support and enhance the design of the foreground figures (see Figure 2.4).

The very nature of leadlight means that the background or 'negative space' has to be cut and broken by lead lines to enable it to be linked with the figures. Although the figures or foreground might be what you actually want to feature in your design, the background too has to be carefully designed so that the whole panel 'flows' and is balanced.

Designing the background so that it allows the figures to stand out while still looking interesting in itself is one of the challenges of designing for leadlights.

Depth

By deliberately creating the illusion of *dimensional space* in your designs you can add a further interesting feature to your work (see Figure 2.4).

Creating depth in your drawings enables you to balance designs backwards and forwards, as well as up and down and from side to side.

Abstract or *geometric* designs especially lend themselves to dimensional effects where the lead lines seem to 'go off into the distance' or are used in a tiered or terraced manner to give the illusion of deep space.

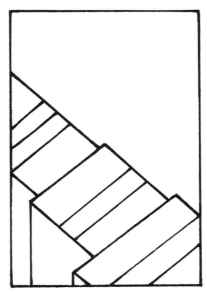

Depth—Creating an illusion of deep space in a design

Space—Background space designed to enhance the subject

Figure 2.4

15

Lines

If you take a pencil and draw a bold horizontal line on a sheet of clean paper you immediately change the appearance of the paper, dissecting it into upper and lower sections.

Lines are an extension of the leadlighter, delivering moods and feelings to a design that are distinctly individual.

'Feel' the line as you draw it and observe what the line does on the blank sheet of paper.

Every line you draw is unique and produces its own special effect, doing something extraordinary to any background you choose to draw it on (see Figure 2.5).

Practise drawing as many different lines as you can think of—thick lines, thin lines, fast lines, slow lines, round, squiggly, sharp . . .

At the same time as you are drawing these lines start trying to make identifiable shapes out of them. Try combining a subject/shape or two within a background.

Use your imagination and don't worry about trying to draw your object too precisely, rather use your lines to *represent* the object, *quickly* and *loosely*, letting the lines flow freely and *concentrating on the line* itself and *where it is* in relation to the background.

Experiment drawing lines using a compass and ruler.

These lines will be harder and less flowing than your freeform ones but will still be very expressive and form interesting patterns, especially dimensional ones.

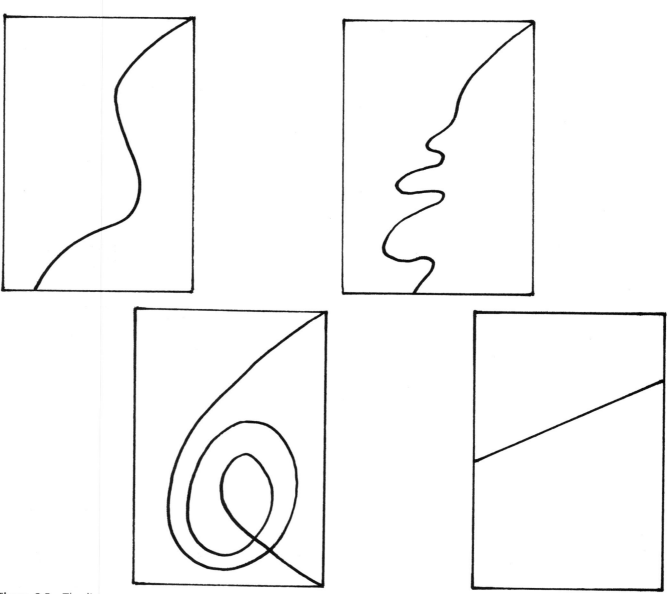

Figure 2.5 The line

Figure 3.1 Colour intensity

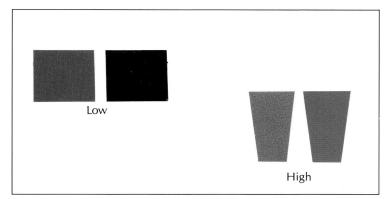

Figure 3.2 Colour value

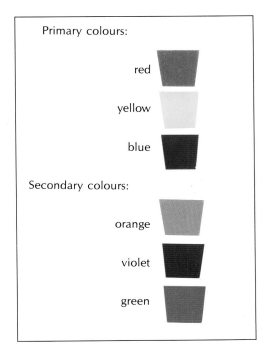

Figure 3.3 Primary and secondary colours

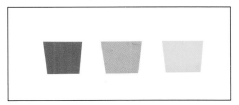

Figure 3.4 Warm colours

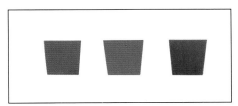

Figure 3.5 Cool colours

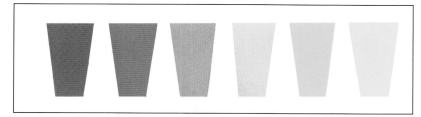

Figure 3.6 Harmonious colours

Figure 3.7 Complementary colours

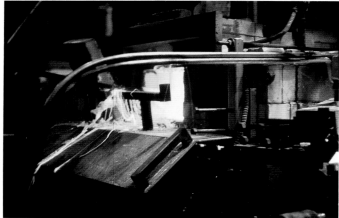

A close-up of the factory ladling bay containing molten glass

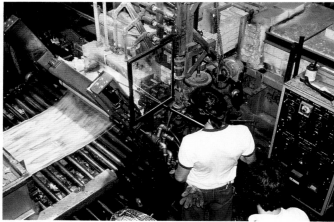

The stirring bay and forming rolls: Glass from the primary and smaller furnaces combines to form a pool (stirring bay). The furnace operator is using a specially designed metal rod to hand-stir the mass, creating swirls to form a multi-coloured glass. A protective window separates the operator from the intense heat while immediately downstream the glass is flowing between two forming rolls, flattening into a glass ribbon

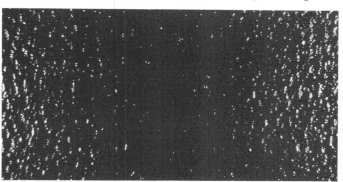

Red cathedral granite-backed glass: Various techniques are used to produce special effects in art glass. Rolled textures are obtained by using an engraved forming roll which imparts a texture on the hot glass as it is formed

Waterglass, shown here in the forming process

Waterglass: This glass has a natural texture and is produced by over-stretching the glass ribbon as it emerges from the forming rolls and is still hot enough to shape

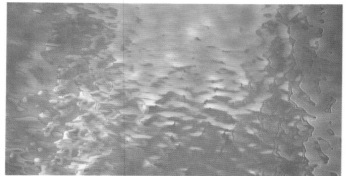

Soft waterglass: This is formed in the same way as regular waterglass but has had fluorine added to the raw chemical composition to give the glass its striking ghostly luminescence

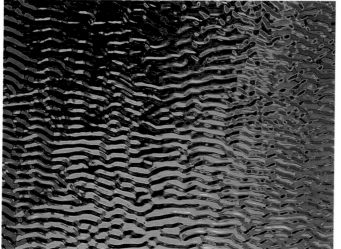

Clear ripple glass: This natural texture is produced by offsetting the speeds of the two forming rolls, setting up a jumpy tension which imparts to the glass this creative effect

18

All photographs on this page courtesy Spectrum Glass

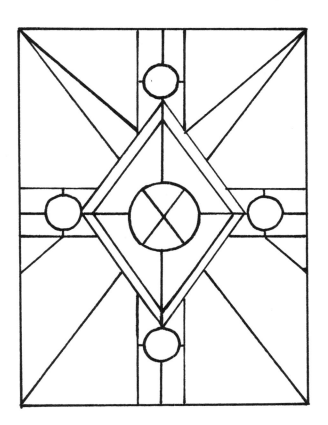

Patterns

Patterns can come either from intuition, or from making use of mathematical repetition.

The repetition of a shape or line is a popular and relatively easy method and is widely used to develop an interesting overall design structure.

Repetition can often be combined with 'one-off' original motifs or figures to create a more visually dynamic work.

3 COLOUR AND LIGHT

Next to design, a leadlight window's single most important visual element is colour.

To fully understand colour one first needs to know about light. In contrast to, say, a painting, which *reflects* light, a leadlight, because it is between the viewer and the source of light, *becomes* the light.

Natural light is the most dramatic and powerful illuminative source for leadlight windows. It can cause dramatic changes in colour as it flows through the glass, radiating and spreading.

Maximum effectiveness and interaction of glass and design in a leadlight window is as dependent on the quality of light available as it is on the actual glass colours used. In the southern hemisphere windows facing the north receive the most even daylight throughout much of the year, as well as throughout each day. The opposite is true in the northern hemisphere. East-facing windows receive the bright morning sun, while windows facing west attract the warm afternoon and red setting sun, as a result undergoing the greatest daily changes. Windows that face south in the southern hemisphere share more in the general changes in daylight than do those that face north. Again the reverse is true in the northern hemisphere.

As light changes it interplays with the coloured glass and its textures, emphasising some colours while causing others to recede visually. For example, blues become more prominent as the light dims, while reds and yellows glow with a brilliance around midday, when the light is at its strongest.

Keep in mind when choosing colours that the lead lines in a leadlight panel form a black frame around each piece of glass. The framing tends to intensify each colour.

Colour has three dimensions

1. Hue This is the term used to identify the name of the colour, e.g. red, blue, yellow, green. Hue is important because of its psychological visual impact. For example, reds are exciting and dynamic; yellows and oranges are cheerful and stimulating; green is restful; blue is serene and spiritual; violet is mysterious.

2. Intensity This term relates to whether the colour (hue) is either bright or dull and takes into account the amount of energy transmitted through the coloured glass (see Figure. 3.1 on page 17).

3. Value The value of a colour is identified between the two extremes, black and white (see Figure 3.2 on page 17). Every colour has a value. Yellow is closer in value to white than is, say, blue.

Each colour also has its variations of value, for example, dark green mixed with white will become light in value. Conversely, a medium green mixed with black would then take on a dark value.

Colours can be used together very effectively when their values are either very close to the dark end of the scale or to the light end. Colours can also work very well and dramatically when their values are contrasting or far apart.

Colour theory is most commonly understood using the three primary colours system. See Figure 3.3 on page 17.

The three primary colours are: red, yellow and blue.

The three secondary colours, obtained by mixing the three primary colours, are orange, violet and green.

All other colours (hues) in between are termed intermediate colours.

Warm and cool colours

Most colours can be categorised as being either warm or cool.

The warm colours, reds, oranges and yellows, tend to advance towards the viewer, visually speaking (see Figure 3.4 on page 17).

The cool colours, greens, blues and violets, tend to recede in the viewer's eye (see Figure 3.5 on page 17).

Violets and greens are often said to be neither cool nor warm as they tend to rely on the colours placed next to them for their expression. For example, green glass next to a blue looks warm, whereas the same green placed next to, say, a yellow, will tend to look cool.

Colour harmony (or unity) is achieved by striking a balanced relationship between hue, intensity and value, while also giving careful consideration to colour areas and to the shapes themselves (see Figure 3.6 on page 17).

One method of producing harmony is through the use of complementary colours (see Figure 3.7 on page 17).

Complementary colours are directly opposite each other on the colour wheel. For example, red is opposite green, orange is opposite blue, purple is opposite yellow.

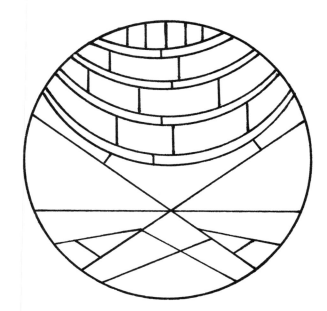

Colour wheels, available from artist's supply shops, are essential for the beginning leadlighter.

Complementary colours used in the right proportions will accent your leadlight panel, providing visual excitement and dramatic highlights.

Analogous colour
This is a colour combination where only two of the primary colours are used in a design, in conjunction with consecutive secondary colours.

Triadic colour
This is a colour scheme where all three primary colours are used.

Monochromatic colour
This is a colour scheme in which only one colour is used, but in variations of values and intensity. Panels designed this way can look low key but strikingly original.

Colour balance
Any colour which dominates a design in hue, intensity or value will tend to overshadow or overwhelm colours of lesser strength. For this reason careful consideration should always be given to the *size* of each coloured area and its actual positioning in the overall design.

How to train your colour sense

The correct use of coloured glass as an art medium requires an understanding of colour and light on the leadlighter's part.

A good colour wheel is important for anyone working in this field. You should always have one with you when you are selecting glass, so that you can readily see which colours go together, and which do not.

It is a good idea to limit your use of different colours to no more than five to begin with, adding a larger range as you become more confident and experienced in colour technique.

Preliminary colour sketches

One excellent way of developing your colour sense is to make several sketches of the leadlight you plan to make and then colour them in different schemes, using either watercolours or oil pastels.

In this way you can experiment, finding which colours work best, avoiding cutting any glass until you're sure of which hues you want to use.

Using a glass easel

When you are satisfied with the colours selected for your design you can move on to the next stage, actually selecting the glass.

For this a glass easel is handy—this is simply a large sheet of clear plate glass held perpendicular in front of a natural light source (i.e. a window) to which the pieces of coloured glass can be attached with Blu-Tack for considered viewing and choice.

To prepare the glass easel, simply attach the design in reverse onto the front. Next, turn the easel over and, using a thick black Texta, draw in the lead lines and border on the glass. The cut glass shapes can be secured within the appropriate pattern areas indicated on the easel.

In this way you will be able to see precisely how your chosen colours go together in a natural light situation, as well as getting a good idea of how the assembled panel will work.

Remember that coloured glass changes in colour from natural light situations to one where artificial (such as fluorescent light) light is used. If your panel is to be backlit by artificial light the cut glass pieces should be viewed over a lightbox for final consideration (see Chapter 5).

A pair of front door panels commissioned for a private residence in Bacchus Marsh, Victoria

A large window commissioned for the dining room of a private residence in Bacchus Marsh, Victoria. The design was reversed in sequence in the five panels for an overall effect

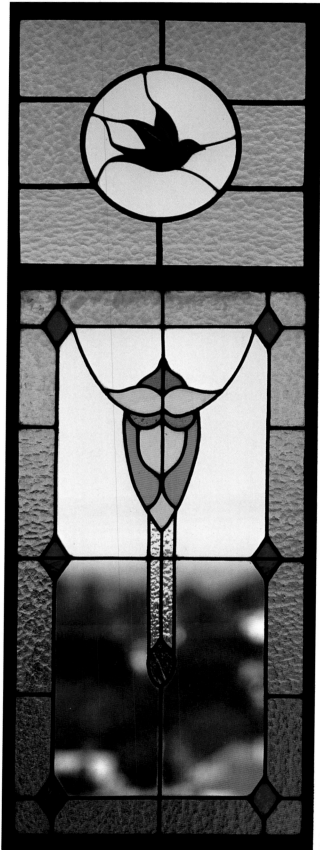

A front door panel commissioned for a private residence in Mount Victoria, New South Wales

One of six panels commissioned for the California Hotel in Katoomba, New South Wales

24

A bathroom window panel commissioned for a private residence in Bacchus Marsh, Victoria

A front door panel commissioned for a private residence in Birchgrove, New South Wales

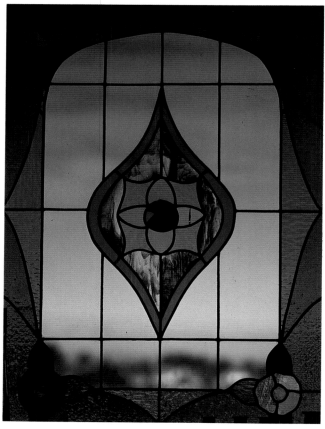

A panel commissioned for the cocktail bar of the California Hotel in Katoomba, New South Wales

This panel was commissioned for a private residence in Carlton, Victoria

4 GLASS

Glass can be compared to the artist's paints.

It is the creative choice of the leadlighter to select those colours and textures of glass that most express what it is they want their finished panel to convey, both visually and in terms of mood.

It is important to remember that at the end of the day your carefully designed leadlight will only be as good as the glass you decide to use in it.

Glass is a catalyst that changes light into a complex mixture of different colour combinations, creating many subtle moods and visual effects. Choosing the glass for your panel should begin as soon as you start working on your design concept. As you look through the sheets of glass, let them influence your ideas and give you further inspiration for the finished window.

Sometimes a particular flaw or a very unusual colour combination in a sheet of glass may suggest a theme or idea for a panel. Use the flaws and thickness variations in the glass to your advantage by featuring them in your work. These unique 'character' pieces will help to make your leadlight work distinctive and highly individualised while at the same time offering creative design features.

As you continually look at and handle coloured glass you will begin to appreciate its very subtle qualities and original ideas will flow as a result. When looking at glass remember to make a mental note of which colours complement each other, which hues belong together and which don't.

Constantly referring to your glass will make you an expert on its best selection; this knowledge will greatly influence and improve your designing.

Glass begins its life in the factory's batch room, where the basic bulk materials of sand, soda and lime are measured. These ingredients, along with alkaline fluxes and stabilising elements, are mixed with various amounts of colouring agents such as cobalt, selenium, manganese and cadmium, according to carefully calculated formulas, to make the numerous coloured glasses commercially available today.

The two basic types of glass used in leadlighting are handblown and machine-made. Handblown (or 'antique') glass is produced by blowing a large cylinder from the molten glass, cutting off the top and bottom and slicing it down one side before it cools. After this it is re-heated into a flat sheet. This type of glass is the most expensive and comes mostly from France, England and Germany. It is characterised by its intense colours and interesting individual textures and faults.

Machine-made glass is rolled out of a machine in a continuous strip. It then goes through cooling ovens before being cut into sheets. It is usually consistent in colour and texture and has an even thickness.

Glass types

The types of glass most commonly used for leadlighting number about twenty.

Cathedral glass
A monochromatic glass, transparent, but because of its texture it usually cannot be seen through.

This was the type of glass used for paintings, nearly all of which were created for church windows, thus it became known as cathedral glass.

Cathedral glass is used extensively for backgrounds in leadlight work. It comes in clears, violets and purple, ambers, greens, blues, reds, yellow and bronze and grey.

Antique glass (mouth-blown)
A term applied to 'art' glass produced by the historic hand-blown cylinder method. Common characteristics of this type of glass include attractive linear patterns and a faultless surface.

Colours available in this type of glass cover the entire spectrum, from delicate pastels to vivid yellows and reds.

Machined antique glass (GNA)
GNA is a machine-made imitation of mouth-blown antique glass. In this process the glass sheet is drawn vertically from the molten state to stretch the surface, giving a glass of excellent quality at a considerably lesser cost than true antique glass.

GNA comes in clear, white, ambers, greens, blues, violets, browns, grey and black.

Flashed glass
A mouth-blown antique glass of clear or light colour with a thin layer of darker coloured glass on one side.

Flashed glass is often used for etching or sandblasting.

This type of glass is available in a range of colours including blue/grey, green, brown, yellow, copper red, pink and purple.

Craquel
To make this glass a hot cylinder of mouth-blown glass is dipped in water, causing radical fissures in the glass.

The cylinder is then re-heated and annealed (toughened) to heal the surface fissures, resulting in an alligator skin-texture.

Textured glass
This is made by double roll forming which produces a glass smooth on one side and textured on the other, thereby allowing an endless number of textured effects.

Granite
This type of glass has a coarse raised and lowered surface similar to a fine gravel texture.

Hammered glass
Hammered glass is distinguished by a uniform texture of raised smooth bumps on its surface which act to diffuse light evenly in all directions.

Baroque glass
A glass featuring a swirly irregular surface; it is available in clear, white opal, pale green, blue, amethyst, cinnamon, champagne, burgundy, topaz, grey, black and white.

Seedy glass
Seedy glass has tiny air bubbles trapped within it. It is made by injecting air or gas into the glass prior to forming while the molten mass is still liquid. It is an excellent background glass in leadlight work.

Iridescent glass
As this art glass is rolled a chemical is sprayed onto its hot surface, resulting in a shimmering film, similar to oil on the surface of water.

Iridescent glass comes in a range of colours, from clear sparkle to black baroque.

Florentine glass
A cathedral glass with a floral-type pattern.

Glue chip glass
A unique glass whose texture is created on the back surface of cold glass by applying hot animal glue. As the glue dries and contracts it chips the surface of the glass in a fern-like pattern. Glue chip glass comes in clear, amber, greens, blue, violet, champagne, red, brown, grey and iridescent.

Streaky glass
Essentially a cathedral-type glass with several colours evident in one sheet; it is also available in textured surfaces. Streaky is available in whites, ambers, greens, blues, violets, champagne and pinks, reds and yellows, grey and black, and also in multi-colour mixes.

Opalescent glass
This is an opaque glass although it will transmit some light. Opalescent glass can be solid or multi-coloured with the colour variation of each sheet being totally unique. The colour range is the same as for streaky glass.

Wispy glass
A clear coloured glass featuring wisps of white throughout, like thin cloud trails.

Waterglass
A clear cathedral glass featuring a non-mechanical, slightly rippled surface of high lustre achieved by stretching the glass during manufacture.

Flemish glass
Flemish glass has a random, undulating wave-like pattern appearing on both sides of the sheet. This type of glass is well suited for backgrounds, borders and geometric pattern features.

Muffle glass
This glass, featuring a subtle star pattern, was extensively used in leadlight windows made in the early 1900s. The pattern was recreated recently for the Australian market.

Texture

As well as being available in many different colours, glass comes with a wide variety of surface textures.

The texture of glass reacts with the light coming through it to create a sparkling effect and great subtlety of hues and tones.

Deliberately contrasting the textures of the glass you use will add enormously to the visual effect of the panel you are creating. This is especially true where you are using very subtle colours, perhaps colours of the same hue, where the required visual contrast can be introduced by using glass featuring interesting or dramatic textures.

5 DESIGNING A LEADLIGHT PANEL

The first thing you need to do when starting out to design a leadlight panel is some considered research on exactly where the proposed panel will go.

Visit the site itself and spend some time looking at the window surrounds and immediate environment.

Is it a modern house the panel is going into?

Or perhaps the building is an older style one?

What aspect does the window space face?

Does the building have a particular mood or atmosphere?

And finally, and this is very important, what is the area and shape of the window space to be leadlighted?

The shape of the window area will dictate the design space you have to work in, and will also aid you in arriving at the most suitable type and shape of design for that particular site.

Some windows are horizontal in area shape while others are vertical (see Figure 5.1)

Whether to use dark or lighter coloured glass will very often depend on how much interior light is readily available without having to resort to using artificial light.

Once you have formulated a rough idea of the design it is time to begin to draw up your panel. It is very important that this is done accurately, taking care to measure the frame opening exactly. Make sure all the square edges in the drawing (cartoon) are exactly square, otherwise the finished panel will be crooked and well nigh impossible to install when completed. Such a badly made panel will also have an embarrassingly lopsided look when viewed.

Not until your panel outline area has been drawn up is it time to start designing. Use a soft lead pencil and try and put down, roughly and quickly, the design ideas you have decided upon and which, so far, are largely visualised in your head.

Use light pencil strokes only to begin with until you can see some good design lines forming. Once you have established some satisfactory lines, go over them in a darker pencil so that they stand out (see Figure 5.2). If you are satisfied with how these darker lines look then go ahead and use them to design around still further, adding new design lines.

The overall process is slow and, at the beginning of the drawing stage, very intuitive. Sometimes, having the initial darkened design lines set out before you, you will begin to add to them in a completely instinctive way, not really sure where the new, lighter lines are taking you.

A fanlight panel commissioned for a bedroom unit in the Central Springs Inn at Daylesford, Victoria

One of a series of four panels commissioned for the dining room of the Central Springs Inn at Daylesford, Victoria

A front door panel commissioned for a private residence in Blackheath, New South Wales

This panel was commissioned for the front door of The Chalet restaurant in Medlow Bath, New South Wales

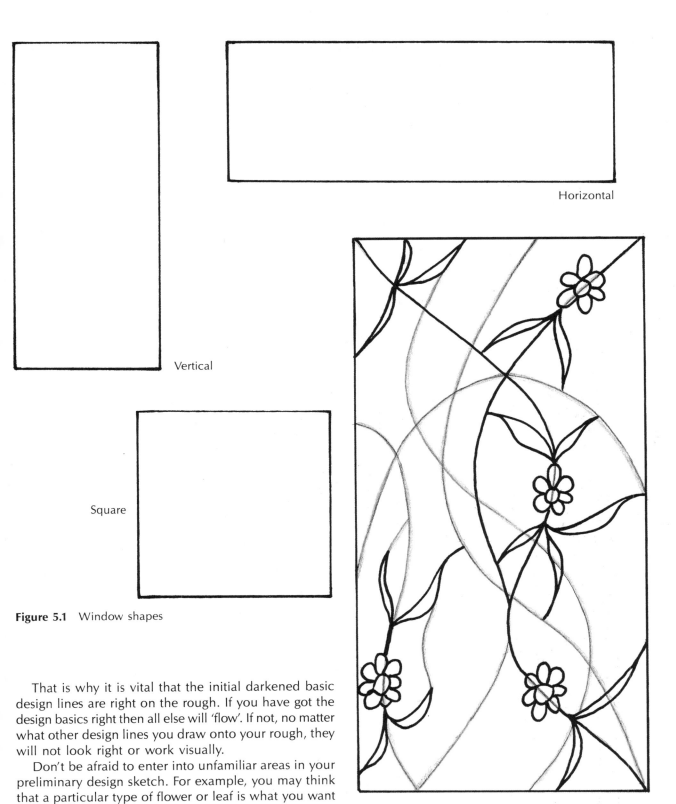

Horizontal

Vertical

Square

Figure 5.1 Window shapes

That is why it is vital that the initial darkened basic design lines are right on the rough. If you have got the design basics right then all else will 'flow'. If not, no matter what other design lines you draw onto your rough, they will not look right or work visually.

Don't be afraid to enter into unfamiliar areas in your preliminary design sketch. For example, you may think that a particular type of flower or leaf is what you want in your design but find that your free drawing produces something quite different. If it looks good leave it in! This is what creative designing is all about. The drawing process can actually alter your own views and concepts and as a result open up whole new areas of design and ways of seeing things.

Figure 5.2 A design in rough state. Note the original lines in pencil. The better of these original pencil lines have been inked in and flowers and leaves added to start to form a pleasing, 'flowing' design. Later, any original pencil lines which are not to be used in the finished cartoon will simply be rubbed out, leaving the desired pattern

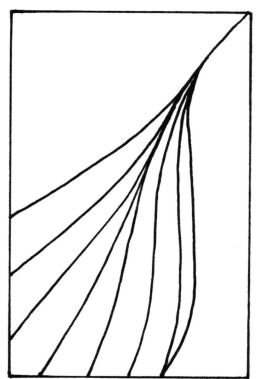

Lead lines all joining at one point, resulting in lumpy joints

Once you have completed your rough drawing to your satisfaction put it on the floor and view it from above to gain a further perspective.

Is it original?

Is it interesting?

Is it balanced?

Does it convey what you wanted, visually?

Does the whole thing work?

If the answers to these questions are 'yes', then carefully draw over the lines in your design in dark pencil, making any modifications as you go. When you have finished you should have your final leadlight design (cartoon) in the rough.

Some people draw their cartoons smaller than the actual window size and scale them up to the actual panel size afterwards. However, unless the window you are planning to make is very large, it is a good idea to make your preliminary rough sketch full size as then you know exactly how the design will look in the given space. Also, by designing full size you can better develop your understanding of the concepts of space, background and foreground and you don't have to change your drawing proportions (as in the case when initial rough cartoons are first done at, say, a quarter actual size).

Once you are completely satisfied with your full size rough design sketch you will need to draw up a second full-sized design, the cutting cartoon. Just before you do this, however, take another look at your finished rough

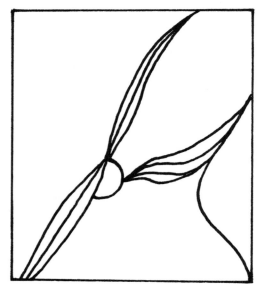

Pieces of glass too thin, resulting in weakness and easy cracking

Design too difficult to cut, curves too tight to cut easily, shapes too narrow for maximum strength when installed

Figure 5.3   Design faults

drawing, paying close attention to all the lines in it. These drawn lines will be your completed panel's lead lines. Check to see how they will look when leaded up.

Are there too many lines joining at the same point which will result in lumpy or untidy leaded areas? (See Figure 5.3.)

Are all the glass areas well supported by lead lines?

Can all of the designed glass shapes be cut out easily?

Are any of the glass shapes too thin and in danger of cracking when assembled?

Will any areas of your panel be too 'leadline dominated' when completed?

Once you have satisfactorily settled these final visual design considerations you can proceed and draw up your second and final cartoon drawing, carefully inking in all lines and borders.

When this has been done overlay the inked-in drawing with a sheet of tracing paper and begin experimenting with your coloured glass selection. If you wish you can make a series of coloured overlays, trying out a wide range of colour combinations. Watercolours give a good impression of glass colours, as do oil pastels.

Selecting your final choice in glass and colours can be done either by viewing each piece of glass against a natural light source (such as a large window) or by making use of an artificial fluorescent lightbox for viewing.

Lightboxes can be purchased from most good leadlight supply shops or, if you prefer and are on a tight budget, you can easily make one yourself, either from an existing box about 230 mm deep, or by constructing one from scratch, using chipboard (see Figure 5.4).

The inside of the lightbox should be painted white to reflect the light which is provided by installing two short

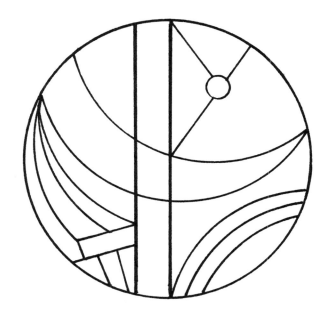

fluorescent tubes in the base. Top the box with a sheet of frosted plate glass, shiny side up. Three ventilation holes should be drilled in the sides to disperse any heat generated by the tubes.

Fluorescent light most closely approximates daylight. Apart from using it to view and select glass, the lightbox is needed when you are cutting darker shades of glass directly over a cartoon. It provides sufficient concentrated light under the drawing to enable you to clearly see the design lines beneath the glass as you cut.

Figure 5.4 Homemade lightbox
1. Plate glass (frosted) cover
2. Holes drilled in the box to disperse tube heat when in use
3. Two short fluorescent tubes attached to the bottom of the box, centred, and approximately 150 mm apart
4. The lightbox should be 200 mm deep and long and wide enough to accommodate the two fluorescent tubes

Note A lightbox can be made from either four-ply or chipboard and should be painted white inside (all surfaces) for maximum light reflection

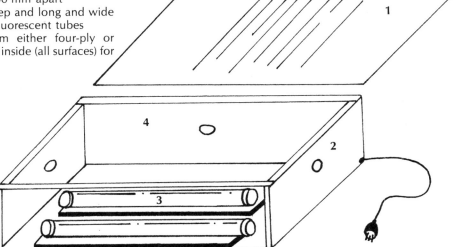

6 SIXTEEN NEW LEADLIGHT DESIGNS

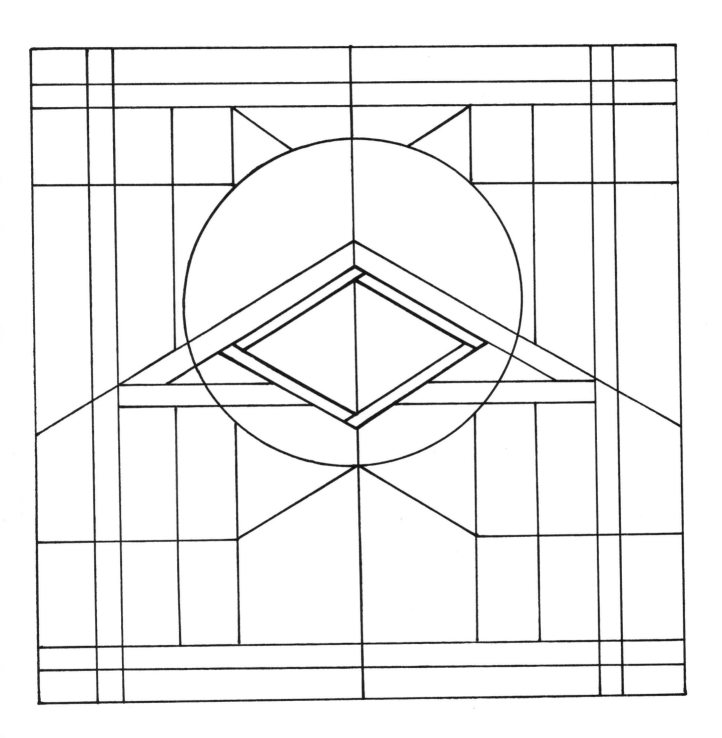

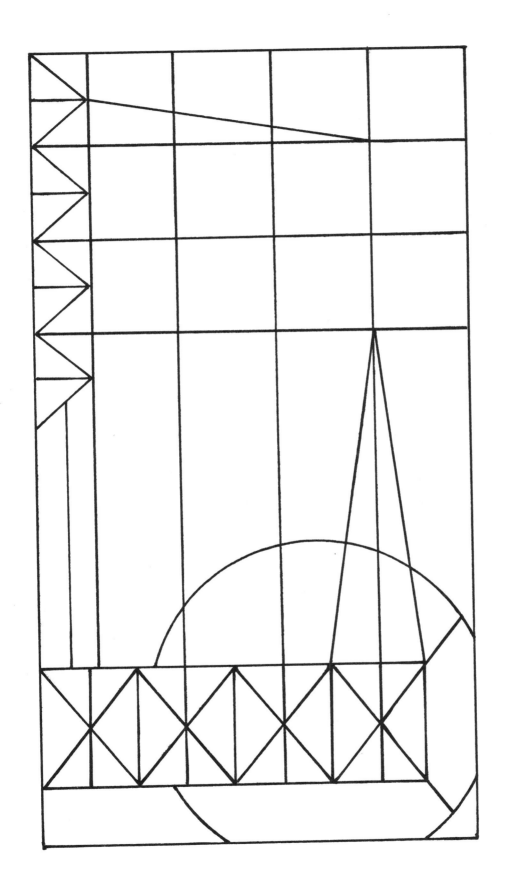

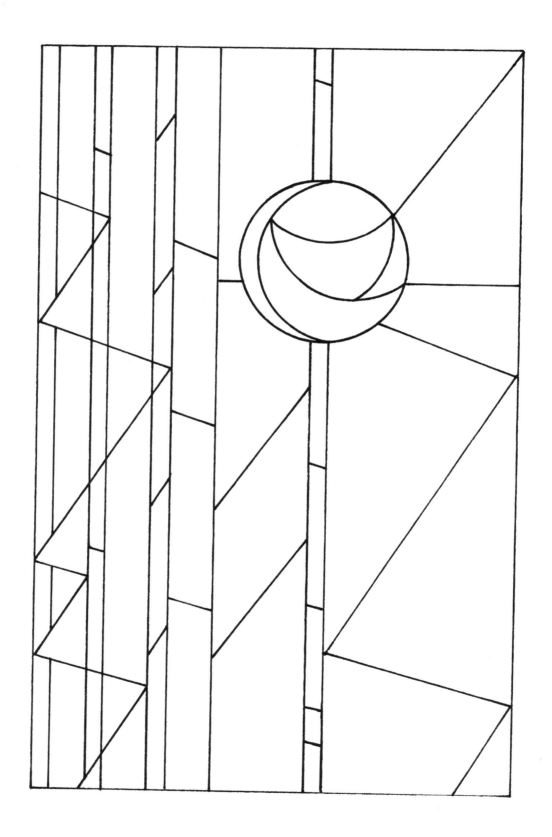

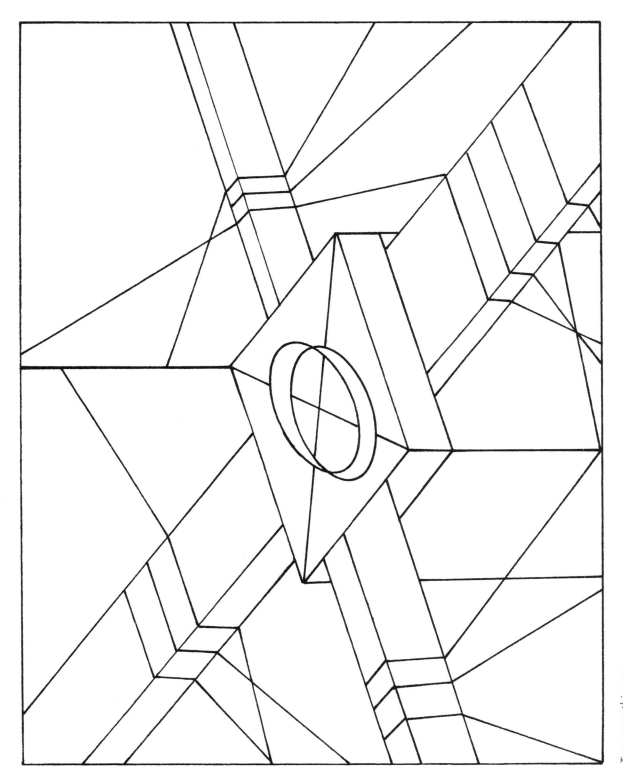

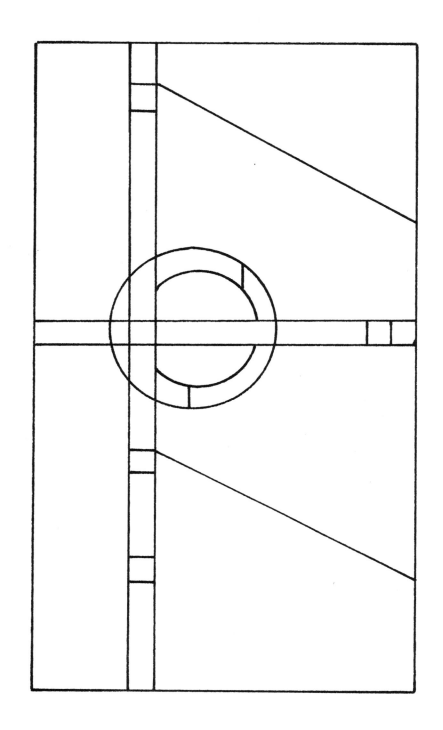

7 THE DRAWINGS BEHIND THE PHOTOGRAPHS

page 23

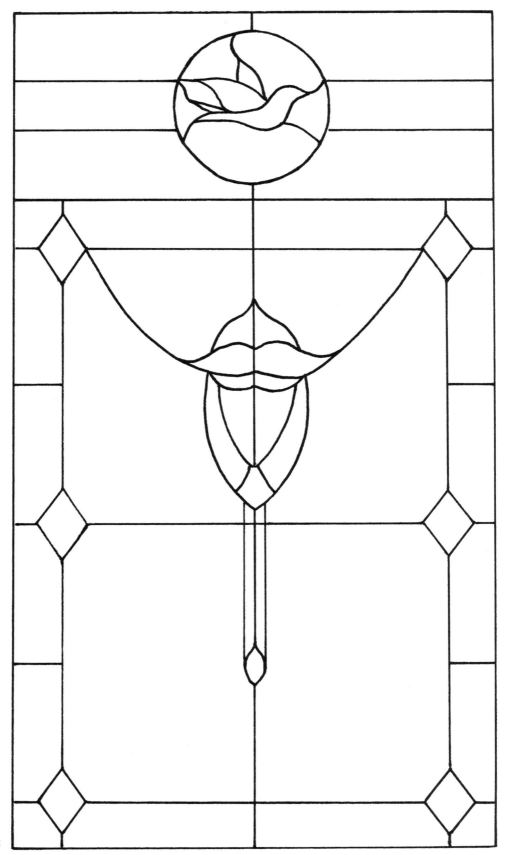

page 25

page 25

page 26

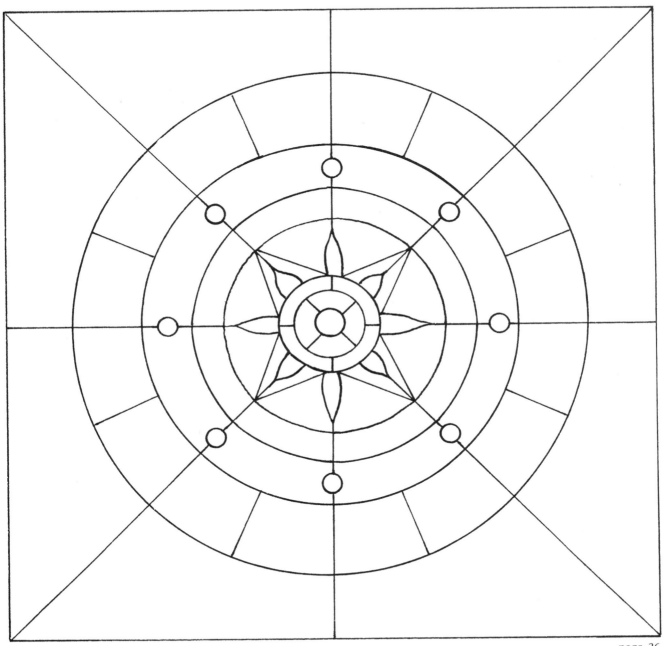

page 26

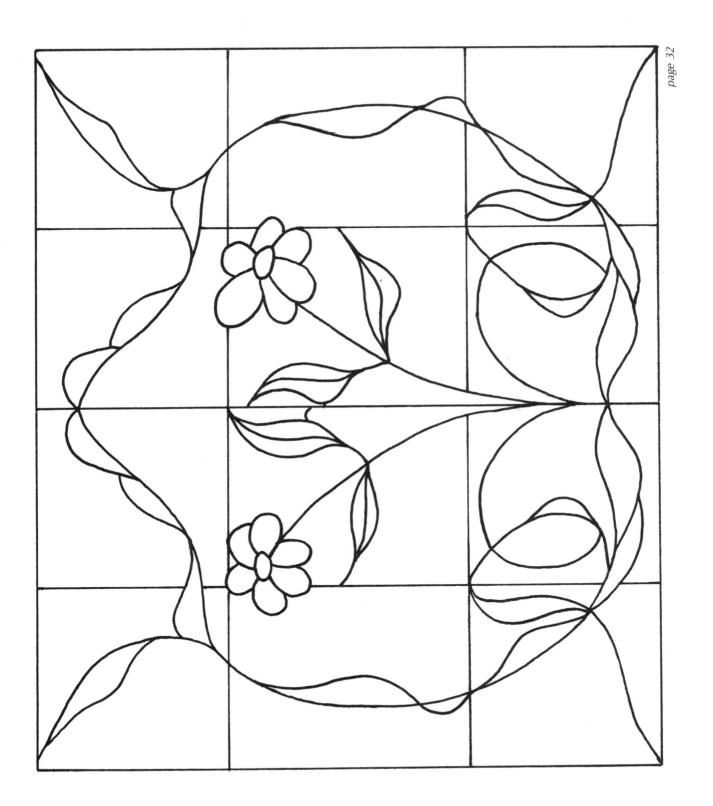

INDEX